Building an Online Foundation for Healthcare Industry

By: Jonathan Hurte and Patrick Fellers

Copyright © 2011

Copyright © 2011 by Patrick Fellers & Jonathan Hurte

All rights reserved. This book or any portion thereof may not be reproduced or used in any manner whatsoever without the express written permission of the publisher except for the use of brief quotations in a book review.

Registered at the US Library of Congress, Copyright Division, # TXu001768763.

Printed in the United States of America

First Printing, 2011

ISBN 978-1-105-15516-1

www.LuLu.com

Table of Contents

Company's Online Identity Intro 4

Establishing and Maintaining a Twitter Account 7

Establishing a Facebook Account 12

Online Article Development, Publication, and Distribution 15

Developing a Newsletter 29

Creating a Virtual Tour DVD 31

Increasing Local Media Coverage 33

Uploading Videos to YouTube 35

Improving Google Ranking 38

Writing and Distributing Online Press Releases 41

Uploading Video and Audio to iTunes 48

Conclusion 54

A Company's Online Identity: the Foundation of Internet Marketing Success

There are many ways to build a company's online platform, some of which include implementing social media, article publishing, article distribution and online press releases. In this introduction, I would like to touch on the aforementioned subjects and how important they are in today's healthcare industry and a company's online identity. I'll explain the steps you can take to build a solid online foundation and enter the world of online marketing with a comprehensive social media platform.

As far as social media platforms are concerned, I am partial to Twitter because of the amount of control a company has as to what information is released to the public via "tweets" (kind of like Blog posts). Twitter currently has over 100 million users worldwide and allows Healthcare companies to communicate quickly, consistently, and effectively with mass numbers of people through short, widely distributed text messages. It is common for a company to have a thousand followers that follow their messages, a good amount of which may be in a related industry. The ability to consistently "tweet" allows an organization to build and expand their online audiences by sharing news, providing information, advertising promotions, and interacting with followers who respond to posted tweets. In addition, Twitter increases a company's existence by enhancing its online presence and web traffic, maintaining daily contact with potential clients/customers, and contributing to the branding of the company as an industry-leading, innovative provider of services. An example of a "tweet", would be a news article by a Social Services representative entitled "Dementia or Simple Forgetfulness?" at http://ezinearticles.com/?Understanding-Dementia&id=4353488.

Facebook is another great social media choice because of its simplicity and over all popularity with all age groups. This is quite important when you are targeting a particular demographic or segment of the population. Facebook allows for two-way communication between your company and prospective clients, employees and/or stakeholders. It is similar to many of the social media platforms in that you may have multiple administrators and individuals that contribute to its rich content. Facebook also ranks quite high in Google search results and provides strong backlinks to a business's website.

The next topic in building an online identity covers article publishing and distribution. As part of its online marketing strategy, a company's expert can write and publish online articles related to their profession and/or the healthcare industry. We do this for three primary reasons:

- Distribution of relevant, healthcare-related articles improves the company image as respected professionals within your field.

- Knowledgeable, well-written articles help establish a company's local affiliates as community experts and trusted resources of information for those seeking to learn more about the topics.

- Online articles, when strategically distributed, help to increase the company's online and community presence. Although these articles are not written as "marketing strategy," they are linked to Twitter, Facebook, Google Site, Website Home Page, iTunes, YouTube, and more which therefore increase traffic and overall Internet presence.

Online Press Releases are written messages directed to members of the media. They are "released" for the purpose of communicating something believed to be newsworthy or informative. Online press releases are distributed to link their news topics and information to mass audiences via the web, social media or other Internet resources. Online press releases are an effective way to increase your company's ranking on search engines like Google, Yahoo, and Bing.

Social media creates a dynamic, traceable, and measurable way to engage your community and drive bottom-line results. Weather its click-through, impressions, videos watched, followers, or "Likes", they all give us an advantage over traditional marketing opportunities in which you can really see how effective your campaign is at any given moment. The benefit to any company is that there is very little capital investment needed to create this strategy.

Establishing and Maintaining a Twitter Account

What is Twitter?

Twitter is one of the world's leading social networking and micro-blogging sites. A blog is an online article. Micro-blogging occurs when users communicate ideas through texts consisting of only a few words, normally no more than one or two sentences. That's 140 characters to be exact.

Users establish Twitter accounts in order to communicate quickly and effectively with other Twitter account holders. Users communicate via Twitter by posting *tweets*. Tweets are brief text messages consisting of no more than 140 characters. Twitter users post tweets that are then read by *followers*. Followers are other Twitter users who have already accepted an online invitation to receive an individual or company tweets.

Why Use Twitter?

Twitter currently has over 100 million users worldwide. Twitter allows company's to communicate quickly, consistently, and effectively with mass numbers of people through short, widely distributed text messages.

By consistently "tweeting," a company can build and expand their online audiences by sharing news, providing information, advertising promotions, and interacting with followers who respond to posted tweets. In addition, Twitter increases notoriety by enhancing its online presence and web traffic, maintaining daily contact with potential clients/customers, and contributing to the branding of the organization as an industry-leading, innovative provider of long-term health care services.

An Example of Twitter's Effectiveness:

Companies have shown how effectively Twitter can be utilized to promote and increase a facility's presence and impact in local communities. A company can build a Twitter following that consists of professionals and organizations in various related industries.

In its first two months of actively pursuing a strong Twitter presence, most companies try to post 300-400 tweets a year with a goal of 1000. These tweets informed followers of a wide arrange of content, including article excerpts, press releases, industry updates, and podcasts, (online video and/or audio broadcasts)

Some companies have maximized their online presence and exposure by tying *ALL* of its web initiatives into its Twitter account. Whenever a company posts a new article, press release, newsletter, or podcast, the organization's Twitter account automatically posts a corresponding tweet.

How to Open an Account:

Step 1: Go to Twitter.com

Step 2: Click "Sign Up" under the "New to Twitter" section

Step 3: Follow the directions to complete sign up

Step 4: The next step will allow you the chance to select **Interests**

Step 5: Select "**Friends**" in your area of expertise or in your market (select "Follow")

Take the time to select and follow as many industry specific people or companies that you can.

How to Post a Tweet:

Step One: Go online to Twitter.com (this will take you to the Twitter Home Page)

Step Two: Click on *Sign In* in the upper right hand corner (this will cause a box to appear that asks for your username or email and password)

Step Three: Type in your *Username* and *Password.*

Step Four: Click on *Sign In* (this will take you to your Twitter Profile Page)

Step Five: Type your tweet in the *What's Happening* box.

NOTE > *Tweets cannot be more than 140 characters.*

Step Six: Click *Tweet* (this will post your tweet to be read by your followers)

NOTE > *The Company should assign someone who is responsible to tweet daily on your behalf, however, you will want to first make sure this person is honest and trustworthy.*

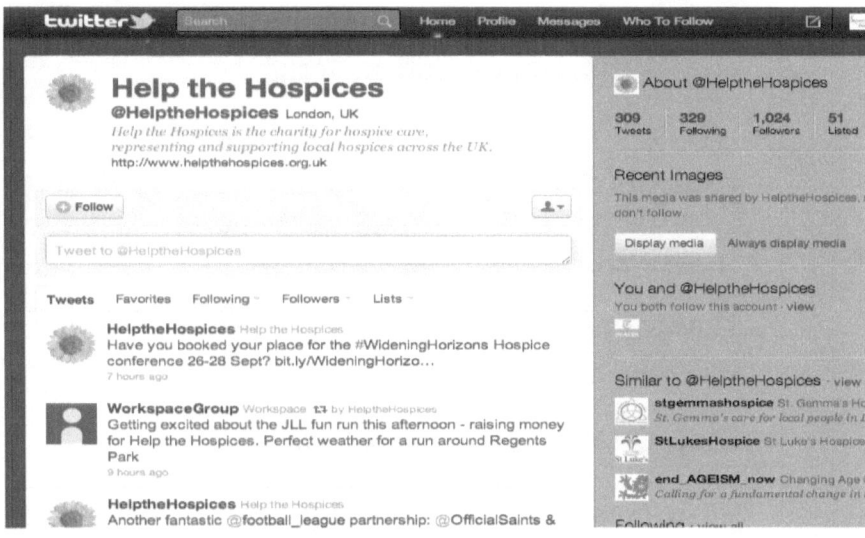

How to Monitor Tweets and Followers:

Step One: Follow steps 1-4 under *How to Post a Tweet* (this should take you to your Twitter profile page)

Step Two: Click on *Followers* in the upper right hand corner, to the right of the *What's Happening* box (this will take you to your Followers Page)

Step Three: Note what followers are posting to tweets. Read and monitor tweets periodically to gauge feedback and to ensure that followers are only posting appropriate material

NOTE > *Check periodically to make sure that twitter posts/tweets are appropriate.*

Creating a Facebook Account –

How to create a Facebook account and get the most out of this social media tool:

Step One: Go to Facebook.com

Step Two: Click on the "Create a page" link on the main page. Select **celebrity, band or business**

Step Three: Click on the company, organization or institution box. Select the industry and type the name of the business. Then click "Get Started"

Step Four: Follow the steps to set up account. The email you want to register, your password and birthday. Also enter the security check word. **Click "Sign Up Now!"**

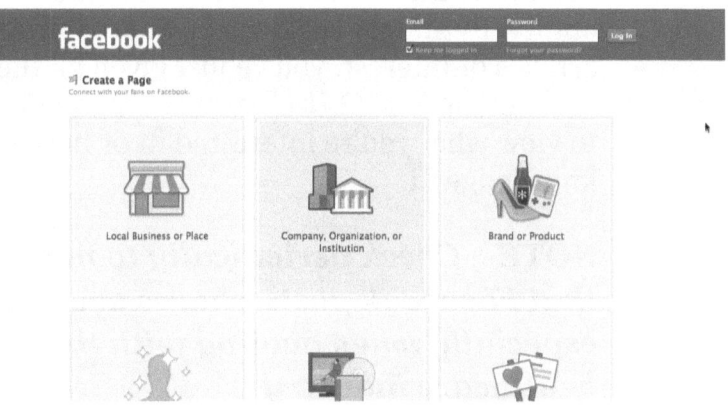

Step Five: Check your email, and find the confirmation. Click the email to complete your registration. The link will lead to the "getting started page." You can look for friends here through email and other methods. Because this account is being created for a business and not a personal account, **do not** complete the "Create your Profile" portion of the application

Step Six: Follow the step by step for your account

Step Seven: Once your account is created...you are far from done. Your first goal at this point is to gather as many "Likes" as you can for your company. Once your company reaches 25 "Likes", it can apply to be the official Facebook site of the company. Your second goal is to produce as much rich industry specific content as possible.

Facebook is the largest most robust online networks. But the one difference is the "Share" ability. By simply clicking the Share button for articles of interest, you've just given all the individuals who "**Like**" your company the potential to view what you're interested in or have expert knowledge in.

NOTE > *Check periodically to make sure that Facebook posts/shares are appropriate especially when dealing with the healthcare industry*

Now you have the ability to share one of your expert articles, YouTube videos, Virtual Tours, Online Newsletters, Twitter posts, etc... and all of the people who "Like" your business have the ability to share this with anyone they are friends with. Every time you reference your website, it adds another valuable backlink to your company's website. More backlinks help in creating a higher Google listing, which in turn leads to more views and more views or clicks can add up to additional exposure to your site. Again, a company will maximize their online presence and exposure by tying *ALL* of its web initiatives into its Facebook account.

NOTE > *Facebook tops Google for weekly traffic in the United States. Also, Facebook added 200 million users in less than a year. Facebook is a powerful social media component*

Online Article Development, Publication, and Distribution

Why Write and Distribute Online Articles?

As part of its online marketing strategy, a company should write and publish online articles related to their industry. We do this for three primary reasons:

First, the distribution of relevant, industry related articles elevates your company image as respected professionals within the industry.

Second, knowledgeable, well-written articles help establish local affiliates as community experts and trusted sources of information for those seeking to learn more about the industry.

Third, online articles, when strategically distributed, help to increase online and community presence. Although these articles are not written as "marketing strategy," they are linked to the companies Twitter, Facebook, Google, Website Home Page, iTunes, and YouTube accounts.

What is the Best Content for Online Articles?

Online articles **should not** be written as marketing pieces. They should not read like commercials or focus on promoting companies attributes and benefits. Many of the best online distribution sites will reject articles that read like advertisements or promotions.

Instead, content should be informative. Articles should focus on a relevant topic or story related to the industry or to some innovative approach being used by the industry to address service and/or needs.

Articles should be original in content and written by individuals affiliated with or contracted by your company. Authors should be knowledgeable and/or passionate about the topics on which they have written. Topics should be adequately researched and appropriate. They should include relevant quotes from notable professionals or individuals.

Below is a sample article written and distributed online by a Healthcare facility:

Change Agent Leadership - Transforming a Skilled Nursing Facility
By Patrick Fellers

One question has been asked of me more times than any other during my career. "How do you transition to a new facility and turn it around so fast?" I have accomplished this task by establishing my role as a "change agent". Being a change agent is what has branded me and my leadership style as I have move from facility to facility over the past several years.

The success of change has many facets. One that makes the most significant change is the concept of supervision leadership. How we supervise and lead is essential to overall operations, staff development, and performance growth.

There are four components that I have practiced, as a leader, in each health care facility that I have operated.

Understanding Human Behavior: This incorporates identifying, implementing, and understanding your own personality as well as the traits and characteristics of others. Through this understanding, you learn how to successfully motivate, encourage and inspire teammates, employees, stakeholders and customers. How many times have you ever worked for someone who treated you poorly, disrespectfully, or through fear? Do you remember how this felt? Do you treat people this way? Look at yourself first. This is self awareness. There are several personality tests you can use or distribute to your staff. You can administer these tests to your team, or hire someone to administer them for you. Either way, you want to know what makes your staff "tick". What makes them wake up every day excited to come to work? What are their work styles? Do they like to work independently or do they work best with a lot of direction? Understanding human behavior is so vast you could spend a lifetime studying the details. As a leader you just need to know the basics. Who you are and who are your staff?

Respect: Say no more, right? You are probably thinking, "That's a given!" Respect is the difference between a successful leader and an unsuccessful leader. Respect is earned, not awarded through academic or career success. Respect by definition is to show or feel honor, hold in high regard, or show consideration for. Humility is a disposition to be humble or lack of false pride. Humility as a leader produces an image of servant leadership. This fabrication generates respect. The respect that is needed to be successful and to promote unity amongst the team is through servant leadership. When you are respected for your work, and you approach your team in a humble manner, you can create an unspoken bond that unites the leaders on your team. Respect and humility combined allows you the opportunity to make mistakes and not be judged. When you are respected by your team, you can progress smoothly in your own work. When you are not respected, you create a divide.

Communication: If you did a Google search today on communication, your search would come up with over 351 million results. For the purpose of making it simple to follow I will touch base on three key areas.

1) Channels of Communication: For me, there are only four of them I focus on: Sender, Receiver, Message, and Feedback. Sender sends the message. The receiver receives the message. And finally the receiver gives feedback so that the sender knows that the receiver received the right message. All four steps are critical. If one is missed, then the communication can and most likely will not be complete.
2) Non-Verbal Communication: What the body, face and eyes express is priceless. You can learn more about how someone is receiving a message by their body language and facial expressions than by any spoken word. And, it is just as important when you meet with someone, you should be aware of not only their expressions but yours as well.
3) Good Listener: Simple. Make eye contact, stop what you are doing, don't interrupt, take notes and paraphrase.

Corrective Action: A corrective action is an attempt to change a behavior, address a weakness in performance, correct a policy violation, or train for enhancement in certain areas. Corrective action is not always written but I would recommend writing down any action that was taken in order to support a pattern. I have witnessed supervisors or leaders fail because they were afraid to practice corrective action. This is a very important tool to be successful as a leader. Help your staff to identify these areas and what steps need to be put in place to correct them. Identifying accountability for one's own actions gains respect for you as a leader, as well as leaders within your facility. This pertains to everyone from you as an administrator to all line staff. Show your own self-respect and humility by openly identifying your own accountability in your own role, and be transparent when you are the one being held accountable for both good and bad. Always address this area with facts, not feelings. Be fair, honest, and consistent. Your goal with any corrective action is to improve performance.

Article Source: http://EzineArticles.com/?expert=Patrick_Fellers

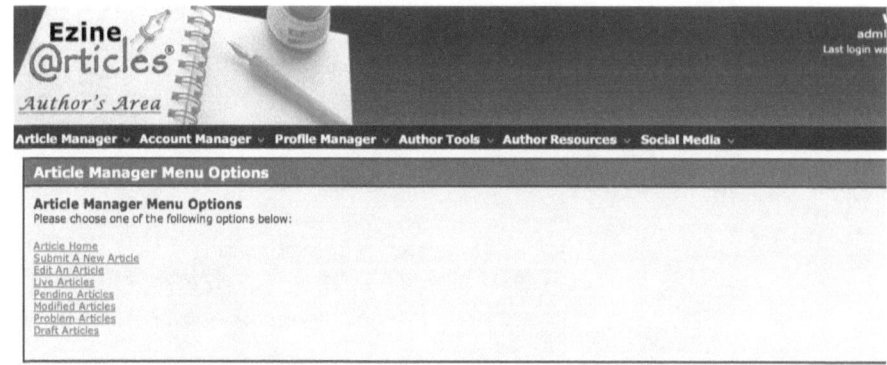

Where Do You Post Articles?

While there are a number of sites through which online articles may be developed, posted, and distributed, we recommend two:

1) Ezinearticles.com

2) Distributeyourarticles.com

Developing and Distributing Articles through Ezine:

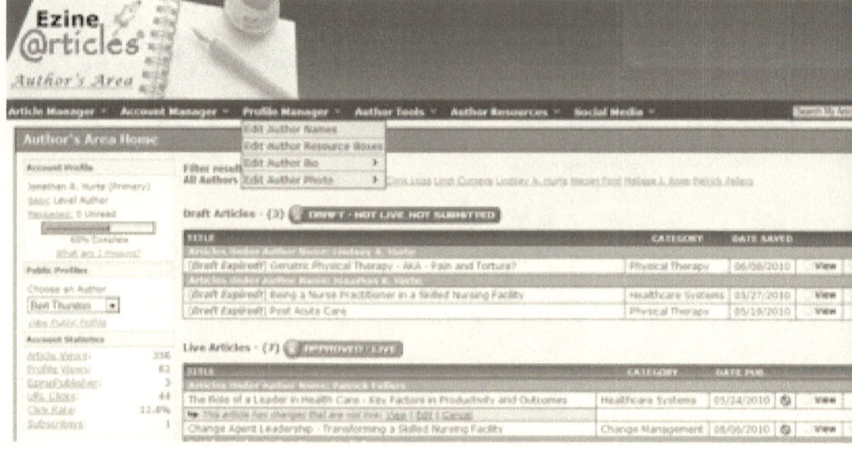

Part 1: Setting Up the Author

Step One: Go to www.ezinearticles.com (this will take you to Ezine Home Page)

Step Two: Click on *Sign In* in the top right of the screen (this will create a box asking for your email and password)

Step Three: Type in your *Email* and *Password*.

Step Four: Click on *Sign In*. Follow the steps to post an article. (this page will also take you to the Author's Area Page)

Step Five: Go to *Profile Manager*, third from left across top of page. (this will create a drop-down box consisting of several options)

Step Six: Click on *Edit Author Names*. (this will take you to the Edit Author Names Page)

Step Seven: Click on *Add an Alternate Author Name*. (this will take you to the Add Alternate Author Page)

Step Eight: Click on the box next to the statement that reads *I agree to the Alternate Author Name Terms of Service*.

Step Nine: Type in the name of the author in the space where it reads *Name to Add* and Click on the arrow next to *Add Alternate Author*. (this will take you to the Author's Bio Public Display Page)

Step Ten: Type in all information regarding the author that the Author's Bio asks for.

NOTE > *the page will ask for your business URL. You should type in your website address in this section.*

NOTE > *Make sure that you include your company Twitter URL. This will enable Ezine to link to your Twitter account when your article is posted.*

Click on *Social Media link*. (this allows you to select your Social Media you want to link to Ezine, then sign in to those pages and follow the directions)

NOTE > *Make sure you authorize access.*

NOTE > Once you have entered information regarding Twitter, make sure you include your company YouTube URL. This will enable Ezine to link to your YouTube account when your article is posted.

- On the Author's Bio Public Display Page, go down to where it says *YouTube URL:,* left side of page

- Click on *Edit This Social Media URL*

- Enter your YouTube URL, then Click on *Update YouTube URL*

Part 2: Submitting the Article

Step One: Follow steps 1- 6. *Part 1:Setting Up the Author*

Step Two: Go to *Article Manager*, upper left

Step Three: Click on *Submit a New Article*. (this will take you to the Submit an Article Page)

NOTE > *you will see direction arrows on the Submit an Article Page. You may click on these arrows at any time to receive additional detailed instructions regarding how to properly submit your article.*

Step Four: Fill out requested article information

- ***Subcategory*** - this is where you pick a subcategory for your article to be posted under

- ***Title*** - this is where you type the title of the article

- ***Abstract /Article Summary*** - this is where you enter a brief summary of the article's subject matter – 200 word limit

- ***Body*** - this is where you enter the text of the article

NOTE > *Articles should be between 500 and 800 words.*

- ***Keywords*** - this is where you enter any words contained within the title and article that you believe potential readers are likely to enter into search engines, such as Google, when they are searching for online material related to your topic/industry.)

- *Author Facility's Box* - this is where you can market your company with some promotional wording. Include a link to your facility's website.)

NOTE > Make sure to include a link to your local website in the *Author Facility's* box.

Step Five: Click on *Preview Article*. (this section allows you to view your article and make any necessary corrections before submitting it to Ezine)

Step Six: Once article is edited and looks good, Click *agree to terms* and Click on *Submit Article*

NOTE > *your article will not automatically be posted. Ezine will first review the article for content to ensure that it is informative and not merely self-promoting. Visit the site within a few days to confirm that your article has been accepted or to address any problems which may have resulted in it being rejected. You can view the status of*

your articles on your Author Areas Page each time you Login (sign in).

Monitoring Articles and Tracking Statistics through EzineArticles.com?

You can track statistics that will help you monitor the distribution and effectiveness of any articles you post through EzineArticles.com.

Step One: Follow Steps 1-4 under *Developing and Distributing Articles through EzineArticles.com.* (this should take you to your Author's Area Page.)

Step Two: Monitor and Review Articles:

- Look under *Draft Articles* to see which articles have not been posted through Ezine and address any issues.

- Look under *Live Articles* to see which articles have been approved and posted through Ezine.

- Monitor various statistics, such as *Article Views*, by Clicking on statistical categories in the *Account Statistics* box located on the left-hand side of the page.

Developing and Distributing Articles through Distributeyourarticles.com:

Part 1: Setting Up the Author

Step One: Go to www.distributeyourarticles.com (this will take you to the Distributeyourarticles.com Home Page.)

Step Two: Type in your ***Username*** and ***Password*** (upper right)

Step Three: Click on ***Login*** (this will take you to your Profile Page.)

Step Four: Scroll down right side and Click on ***Add Pen Name***

Step Five: Fill out ALL requested information

Part 2: Submitting the Article

Step One: Follow steps 1-3 under *Part 1: Setting Up the Author*. (this will take you to your Profile Page.)

Step Two: Scroll down right side and find ***Submit an Article.*** Then, Click on *Basic*. (this will take you to the Submit an Article Page)

Step Three: Fill in ALL required information.

- *Article Title* - this is where you type in the title of the article

- *Article Description* - this is where you type in a brief summary of the article's subject matter

NOTE > *The Article Description cannot exceed 400 words.*

- *Article Body* - this is where you type and/or paste the text of the article

NOTE > *The body of the article should be between 700-800 words.*

NOTE > <u>DO NOT</u> submit the same article to both Distributeyourarticles.com and EzineArticles.com. Search engines will recognize the article as a duplicate and your articles will get "<u>kicked out</u>." You may submit articles addressing the same topics and/or by the same author, but the text needs to be different.

- *About the Author* - this is where you type a brief biography of the author

NOTE > *This section should not exceed 500 words.*

NOTE > *You will want to include relevant URLs (your company website address, Twitter URL, YouTube URL, etc...) in this section.*

- ***Categories / Subcategories*** - this is where you choose a category and/or subcategories for your articles

- ***Keywords*** - this is where you enter any words contained within the title and article that you believe potential readers are likely to enter into search engines, such as Google, when they are searching for online material related to your topic/industry

Step Four: Scroll down and review the article, correcting any mistakes and making any necessary edits

Step Five: Once article is edited and looks good, Click *agree to terms* and Click on *Submit for Review*

NOTE > *Your article will not automatically be posted. It will first be reviewed for content. Visit the site within a few days to confirm that your article has been accepted or to address any problems which may have resulted in it being rejected.*

Viewing and Checking on the Status of Articles on Distributeyourarticles.com:

Step One: Follow steps 1-3 under *Part 1: **Setting Up the Author***. (this will take you to Your Profile Page)

Step Two: Scroll down right side and Click on ***View My Articles***. (this will take you to your View All Articles in My Account Page)

Step Three: Review the status of your articles to ensure that they are being distributed and/or to address any issues preventing their distribution.

Developing a Newsletter (Hard and Soft Copy)

Why Develop a Newsletter for Your Company?

A newsletter is an effective way to market to both an internal and an external audience. Externally, a newsletter serves to promote the company and emphasize its presence in the community by highlighting events, success stories, articles, announcements, professional accolades, the organization's philosophy and vision, and so on. Internally, it can boost employee morale, build unity, provide inspiration, highlight exceptional residents and staff members, and communicate key information to members of the organization. These Newsletters may also be posted on Facebook and Word Press website page.

How to Publish an Effective Newsletter:

Step One: Once your computer is on, Click on *Start* (usually lower left)

Step Two: Under *Programs*, Click on *Microsoft Word*. (you may only need to scroll up to find Microsoft Word once you have clicked on ***Start***)

Step Three: Click on the ***Newsletter Template***

Step Four: Insert written text in the appropriate areas

Step Five: Insert desired pictures in the appropriate areas

Step Six: Save as a PDF file when finished

- Click on ***Save As***

- Click on ***PDF***

- Click on ***Publish***

NOTE: We have found it actually more cost effective to use an outside printing resource company.

Creating a Virtual Tour DVD

What is a Virtual Tour?

Virtual tours are videos that allow potential customers an opportunity to get a visual glimpse of your company without having to actually be on the premises. Most businesses will produce two videos. The first is a ***Short Tour (At a glance).*** The short tour video simply features pictures of the company with music of choice added.

The second is a ***Full Tour***. The full tour video features a more in-depth view of the company, as well as interviews, and a deeper explanation of the company's philosophy when it comes to the industry (i.e. mission and vision statement, stakeholder and customer testimonials).

Why Produce Virtual Tour DVDs?

Virtual tours can be effectively utilized in several ways. First, they provide a resource for potential customer to view the company without having to actually visit. Customers who live in another city or out of state can take an online tour to better know if the company meets their needs.

In addition, since company virtual tours can be viewed via YouTube, iPhones, Facebook, Companay Website, Androids, and so on, they can be viewed from almost anywhere at any time. Company representatives need not simply rely on word-of-mouth or traditional marketing materials to share with the industry and potential customer the benefits of your company. They can literally *show them* no matter where they are, via a virtual tour. Many companies are now loading all of this technology onto tablets (like iPads), so that they are able to showcase the company at any time with little to no preparation involved.

Finally, virtual tours provide an additional marketing tool to individuals visiting the company website. Your company can have a virtual tour playing in your waiting room or in a conference room to mark the beginning of an actual onsite tour. DVDs can also be given as gifts or as part of informational packets to visitors who have visited the company. Potential customers do not need a computer to view your companies Virtual Tour DVDs. They can be played on any standard DVD player.

How Do We Produce a Virtual Tour DVD?

Our company can assist you in producing your DVDs and will train you in how to effectively post them online. Your company simply incurs the cost of production and distribution. Current quotes for bulk production are approximately $3.00 per DVD – consulting fees may apply if necessary.

NOTE > It is important to make sure that you have obtained legal permission before filming. (this can be accomplished using a standard Media Release legal document)

Increasing Local Media Coverage

This section addresses practical steps your company can take to increase your organization's local media coverage and enhance its reputation in the community.

1) Join Your Local Chamber of Commerce:

The Chamber of Commerce provides various networking opportunities and enables your company to establish relationships with key business leaders and organizations in your community. The key to utilizing your local chamber of commerce is to attend functions consistently and, when possible, participate in chamber-sponsored/related events.

2) Become Involved in Community Projects:

Participate in and help sponsor key community events: Charitable events, 5k runs, community days, events that are meant to educate the community about industry topics, etc. Become active participants in civic organizations, participate in community outreach projects, and so on.

3) Sponsor Community Events:

Whenever possible your business should volunteer, sponsor, or host community events. It is especially beneficial for your business to sponsor events directly related to industry, such as walk-a-thons, special events for families and kids, educational events aimed at improving health, and so on.

Uploading Videos to YouTube

What is YouTube?

YouTube is a website through which people, businesses, and organizations can upload, share, and view videos. YouTube is currently ranked as the world's #2 online search engine. Only Google ranks higher. (Google now owns YouTube.) YouTube has over 300 million visitors and roughly 5 billion video streams per month (40% of all videos online). Recent estimates show that approximately 15 hours of video are uploaded to YouTube every minute!

Why Upload Videos to YouTube?

Due to its popularity as a search engine, YouTube affords businesses like yours the opportunity to communicate visually with millions of potential viewers. It also increases your facility's exposure by increasing its online presence and making your information accessible via the world's #2 search engine.

Recent studies show that websites featuring and/or linked to videos are 80% more effective in drawing web traffic than sites that have no video and/or are not linked to video sites like YouTube. Uploading videos to YouTube is an effective way to make virtual tours, promotional messages, and topical videos accessible to millions of potential online viewers.

NOTE > *It is important to make sure that you have obtained legal permission before filming* **(this can be accomplished using a standard Media Release legal document)**

How to Upload Videos to YouTube:

Step One: Go to www.youtube.com

Step Two: Click on *Sign In*, upper right. (this will this will take you to the sign in page)

Step Three: Type in your *Username* and *Password*

Step Four: Click on *Sign in* (this will take you to your facility's account)

Step Five: Click on *Upload*, top center

NOTE > *after completing step five, you will be given the option of connecting to your social media accounts. You want to make sure that you do link to them.* <u>VERY</u>

_IMPORTANT__: Make sure you enable your connections._

Step Six: Click on **_Connect_**. (this will connect your video to your social media accounts)

Step Seven: Enter all required information regarding video

Step Eight: Click on **_Upload Video_**

Step Nine: Click on the video in your computer files which you wish to upload to YouTube

NOTE > **_Videos may not exceed 2 gigabytes (2 gb) in size and may not be longer than 15 minutes in length._**

NOTE > **_Make sure to use a descriptive title that includes the name of your company._**

Step Ten: Enter details in appropriate spaces

- Detailed written description of the video

- Choose a tag. (what topic/category is the video found under?)

    For Example: Nursing Home, Retirement Home, Facility's Healthcare, long-term health care, etc.

Step Eleven: List your video under *Public* rather than private

Step Twelve: Add your URL (website address)

Step Thirteen: Click on *Upload*

Step Fourteen: Wait for your video to upload (this could take a few minutes)

Step Fifteen: Click on *Save Changes*

Improving Google Ranking

What is Google?

Google is a multinational Internet search, computing, and advertising corporation. Most notably, Google ranks as the number one search engine in the world.

Why is a Strong Google Ranking Important?

The vast majority of online users rely on Google as the search engine through which they surf the Internet. Studies show that 80% of Google users will not scroll past the first two pages when seeking a service provider. Therefore, it is imperative that your company rank as high as possible on Google, especially in your local market.

How to Edit / Improve Your Google Place Page & Ranking:

Step One: Go to www.google.com (this will take you to the Google Home Page.)

Step Two: In the rectangular box, type "your business [your city]."

Step Three: Click on *Google Search*. (this will take you to a Google search page that should include your company's place page as an option. [Your Place Page option normally displays a map showing the location of your business.])

Step Four: Click on *Place Page* (this will take you to your company Place Page)

Step Five: Click on *Edit This Place*, top of page, slightly right of center

Step Six: Click on *Edit Business Information* (this will allow you to make any desired changes to your company's Google Place Page)

> For Example: You can change business owner/management information, demographics, statistics, etc.

Step Seven: Click on *Continue*

NOTE > It is very important for purposes of search engine optimization (improving your Google ranking) that you FILL OUT ALL INFORMATION and that you keep at least eight pictures and/or videos on your profile. THE MORE RELEVANT INFORMATION YOU PROVIDE ON YOUR PLACE PAGE, THE HIGHER YOUR GOOGLE RANKING TENDS TO BE.

Step Eight: Once you update your information, Google will ask you how you want to verify your changes. It will give you two options: 1) Send Postcard; or 2) A Phone Call. The quickest means of verification is to choose the phone call option. However, if your phone number is for some reason incorrect on your profile, then the postcard option is fine.

NOTE > *If you choose the postcard option, it may be two weeks before Google mails you verification. When it arrives, the postcard will provide you with:*

1. A website to go to

2. An account I.D.

3. A password

4. A PIN #

NOTE > *Regardless of which method of verification you choose (phone or postcard), Google will take up to six weeks to process and actually update your information.*

NOTE > *You can also monitor online reviews of your facility through your Google Place Page. Simply follow steps 1-4 under How to Edit / Improve Your Google Place Page and Ranking. Then, Click on Reviews, located just below your company name and address on your Place Page.*

Writing and Distributing Online Press Releases

What is an Online Press Release?

Press releases are written messages directed to members of the media. They are "released" for the purpose of communicating something deemed to be newsworthy or informative. Online press releases are distributed online.

Why Issue Online Press Releases?

Online press releases allow you to distribute the news and information to mass audiences via the worldwide web. Online press releases are an effective means by which to increase your companies ranking on search engines like Google, Yahoo, and Bing. Online press releases also enable you to post news stories concerning your business to major online media sites like Google News, Yahoo News, and Topix.

Issuing Press Releases through PRweb:

PRweb is an online site that specializes in distributing online press releases to a mass number of sites. Upon approval of your content, PRweb will distribute your press release to over 250,000 subscribers, 30,000 websites, and roughly 30,000 bloggers and journalists. Such mass exposure boosts your organization's online presence and increases the likelihood that readers will view your press release and visit your site.

Example of the Effectiveness of Online Press Releases:

In 2010, a Healthcare facility utilized PRweb to effectively distribute online press releases. The facility's first two releases were each picked up by

Yahoo News and Topix. The first release received over 1000 reads. The second received over 1700.

What's the Best Content for a Press Release?

Online press releases should not read like marketing pieces. They should not focus on promoting your company. Rather, they should be informative and newsworthy. Possible topics include:

- A special event involving your business and/or your stakeholders.

- An innovative approach to your business.

- An award or special recognition bestowed upon your business by an outside organization or institution

(Below is a sample press release issued by Healthcare facilities and distributed via PRweb):

How to Issue an Online Press Release via PRweb:

Step One: Go to www.prweb.com

Step Two: Click on *Login*, upper right (this will take you to the Login Page)

Step Three: Type in your *Email* and your *Password*

Step Four: Click on *Login* (this will take you to your My PRweb Page)

Step Five: Click on *Create Release*, third from left across the top of the page (this will take you to the My Releases Page)

Step Six: Under *Basic*, Click on *Select Now* (this will take you to the Choose Your Distribution Enhancements Page)

NOTE > *In most cases, you do not need to add any additional enhancements.*

Step Seven: Click on *Next – Payment*, bottom right (this will take you to the Payment Page)

Step Seven: Fill out relevant payment information

Step Eight: Click on *Submit Payment* (this will take you to the page where you will construct and submit your press release.)

Step Nine: Fill out information for your press release.

- *Title* - this is where you will type the title of your press release

- ***Summary*** - this is where you will type a brief summary regarding the subject matter of the press release

- ***Body*** - this is where you will enter the text of your press release

- ***About Author*** - this is where you will enter a brief biography of and/or relevant information regarding the author. You can also upload a picture. Make sure to include the URL [website address] of your specific facility

Step Ten: Click on ***Submit Release*** (this submits your press release to PRweb)

NOTE > Upon submission, PRweb will review your release to make sure that its content meets proper standards for mass distribution (i.e. is informative rather than reading like an advertisement). If your release is up to standard, it will be distributed beyond PRweb to Yahoo News. If not, it will only be available on PRweb.

NOTE > It is <u>VERY IMPORTANT</u> that you make sure your press releases are worded in such away so as to be approved for distribution to Yahoo News. Yahoo News reaches millions of viewers and can

potentially offer hundreds of backlinks to your website. *Backlinks* are incoming links to your facility's website. The more backlinks your site has, the more visitors it will likely get and the higher your facility's site will rank on search engines.

How to Monitor the Effectiveness of Your Press Releases:

Step One: Follow steps 1-4 under *How to Issue an Online Press Release via PRweb*

Step Two: Click on *Analytics*, fourth from left across the top of the page. (this will take you to a Summary Page with graphs and/or charts tracking exposure and distribution)

Step Three: Monitor your press release

- Click on *Reads*, to the left under "Summary," in order to monitor the number of reads.

- Click on *Traffic Sources*, to the left under "Summary," in order to monitor which sites are producing the most reads AND what keywords viewers are entering into search engines that led them to your release.

Uploading Video and Audio to iTunes

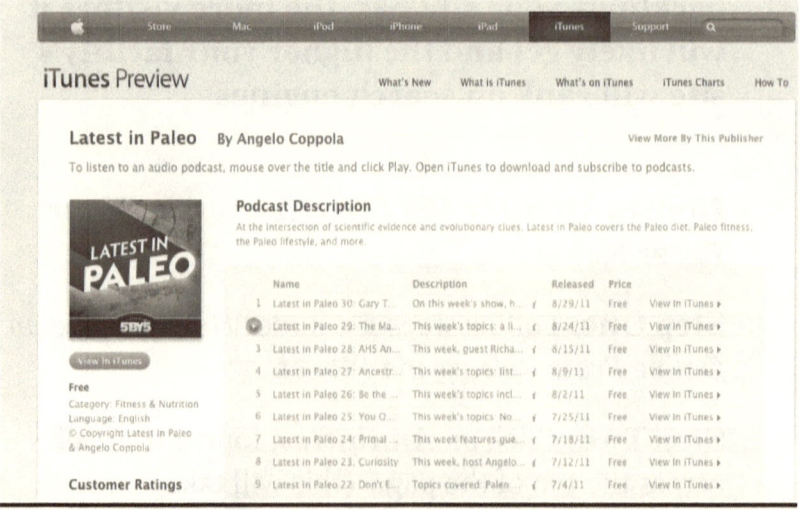

What is iTunes?

iTunes is a website that allows individuals and businesses to upload and download video and audio messages. *Podcasts* (online video or audio broadcasts, often released episodically) and *vodcasts* (online video productions) continue to grow in popularity because they allow users to communicate online via actual audio commentary and/or visual demonstrations and images rather than simply via text.

Why Use iTunes?

ITunes allows you to promote your business in an effective, innovative way. Because iTunes allows you to distribute information through audio and video, your company is able to share relevant lectures, tours, testimonials, powerful images, and so on that can potentially captivate viewers' interest. With roughly 5 million visitors per day, iTunes allows you to reach and educate viewers who might otherwise not inquire about your services. This increases the number of visits to your website, potentially multiplying your company's impact while expanding your business.

How to Upload Audio / Video Files to iTunes via Podbean:

NOTE > *The following directions are given with the assumption that you have video and/or audio files capable of being uploaded to iTunes (i.e. -- .MOV, .AVI, .WMV, .MP3, .MP4, etc)*

Step One: Go to www.podbean.com

Step Two: Click on *Login*, upper right (this will take you to the Login page.)

Step Three: Type in your *Username* and *Password*

Step Four: Click on *Login* (this will take you to your company's Podbean Home Page.)

Step Five: Click on *Publish Podcast*, top center (this will take you to the Dashboard Page)

Step Six: Click on *Upload*, second from top left (this will take you to your Media Manager Page)

Step Seven: Once on Media Manager Page, you will need to Click on *Start* in the bottom left-hand corner of your computer screen (not part of the website). (this will cause the Start Menu to appear on your screen)

Step Eight: Move your computer mouse to where it says *Programs* or *All Programs*. Without having to click, the screen should display a menu of your computer's available program files

Step Nine: Scroll up Program Menu until you come to file named *FileZilla*

NOTE > *You should download FileZilla onto your system to ensure that this program is available.*

Step Ten: Click on *FileZilla* (this should open the FileZilla file.)

Step Eleven: Use FileZilla to upload video / audio file to Podbean

Step Twelve: Close FileZilla. Screen should return to Media Manager Page on website. If not, repeat steps 1-6 above

- Look under *Current Media Files* section of Media Manager Page to confirm that the file you uploaded has, indeed, been successfully uploaded to Podbean.

NOTE > *Now that your video / audio file has been uploaded to Podbean, it is time to publish it on iTunes.*

Step Thirteen: On Media Manager Page, Click on *Publish*, upper left (this will take you to the Write Post / Episode Page)

Step Fourteen: Type in information asked for by website regarding your podcast

- *Tag:* This is where you will type in relevant key words.

- *Title:* This is where you will enter the title of your podcast.

- ***Post***: In this section, you will type a brief description of the subject matter that your podcast pertains to.

Step Fifteen: On Write Post / Episode Page, go under *Podcasting* section at bottom of page. Under Add *Media File:* Click on ***Select from Account*** box. (A drop box will appear featuring a list of files from which you may select)

Step Sixteen: Scroll down and Click the video file you want to upload to iTunes

Step Seventeen: Under ***Add Media File*** Click on the *Video **Preview Image*** box (a drop box should appear)

Step Eighteen: Scroll down and Click on *the jpg*.

NOTE > Step Eighteen is important because it ensures that it is your company logo rather than Podbeans that will accompany your audio/video.

Step Nineteen: Click on ***Save***, lower right

Step Twenty: Click on ***Publish***, lower right (this should send your audio / video file to iTunes)

NOTE > ***It will take iTunes at least 24 hours to publish your video online.***

How to Check the Status of Your iTunes Audio / Video Posts:

Step One: Click on ***Start***, lower left corner of your computer screen (this will cause the Start Menu to appear on your screen)

Step Two: Scroll up Menu until you come to *iTunes* and Click on the program (this should open iTunes)

Step Three: Click ***Podcasts***, top of page

Step Four: Type in password. (This should produce a list of your audio / video files that are currently on iTunes)

Step Five: Click on the file that you wish to make sure uploaded correctly

How to Link Your iTunes Podcasts & Vodcasts to Twitter and Facebook:

Step One: Follow steps 1-3 under *How to Check the Status of Your iTunes*
      Audio / Video Posts.

Step Two: On the iTunes Home Page, Click on the *Free* box (this will create a drop-down box)

Step Three: Scroll down and Click on *Share on Twitter* (this will link your iTunes podcast to your Twitter account)

Step Four: Scroll down and Click on *Share on Facebook* (this will link your iTunes podcast to your Facebook account)

Conclusion:

There are many different options for a business or organization as far as social media and Internet identity options. We have focused on the mediums of marketing and online identity that give you the most effective and well-rounded healthcare marketing solutions. Again, the keys to success is to promote and increase a facility's presence and impact in local communities, increase a company's overall Internet impression, and elevate your image as respected professionals within the healthcare industry. A large part of building a solid Internet platform is getting recognition, exposure, and credibility. Lastly, a company's online identity is measurable way to engage your community and drive profit driven results. We hope this manual gets you pointed in the right direction helps you achieve your goals with Internet marketing. Good luck!

www.ingramcontent.com/pod-product-compliance
Lightning Source LLC
Chambersburg PA
CBHW021925170526
45157CB00005B/2192